# The Making of The 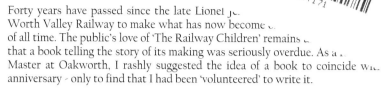 ~n

*Compiled for the Keighley & Worth Valley* ey

Forty years have passed since the late Lionel Jc. / and
Worth Valley Railway to make what has now become ᴄ. / films
of all time. The public's love of 'The Railway Children' remains ᴄ. ɔng felt
that a book telling the story of its making was seriously overdue. As ᴀ . Station
Master at Oakworth, I rashly suggested the idea of a book to coincide wᴛᴄ. .lm's 40th
anniversary - only to find that I had been 'volunteered' to write it.

Many long-standing volunteers kindly raided their attics and I soon assembled hundreds of photographs and recorded many memories on my aged cassette tape recorder. This book therefore stands as a tribute to those pioneering volunteers of 40 years ago and the knowledge and inspiration they continue to pass on to their successors. In particular I would like to thank Brian Baker, Bill Black, Peter Eastham, Mike Goodall, Ken Hastwell, Nick Hellewell, Robin Higgins, Chris Lawson, Robin Lush, Howard Mais, Howard Malham, Graham Mitchell, David Pearson, Eric Ring, Ken Roberts, Ian Walker and Martin Welch. Thanks are also due to BBC World, Bradford Telegraph & Argus, Optimum Releasing, Yorkshire Post Newspapers and Haworth Band for their valuable assistance in the production of this book.

Advancing years can play tricks with one's memory so some of the contributors' recollections may be a bit vague in places. However they remain an invaluable addition to this Railway's history and its proud contribution to what remains a very fine British film.

Published by the Keighley & Worth Valley Railway Preservation Society, The Railway Station, Haworth, Keighley, West Yorkshire, BD22 8NJ.

Copyright – Keighley & Worth Valley Railway Preservation Society 2010

First published March 2010

ISBN: 978-0-902438-33-0

Photo: Robin Higgins

*This book is dedicated to*
*'Tabitha'*

# "We were not Railway Children to begin with"

BOB CRYER recalls ..........................

The late Bob Cryer worked as Railway Consultant to the film makers and wrote this article shortly after the film's release. Bob was one of the Railway's founder members and spent some time as Keighley MP, a role currently held by his widow, Ann Cryer.

Photo: Telegraph & Argus, Bradford

**To Begin at the Beginning** - The feature film of Edith Nesbit's charming story did not simply spring into being in 1970; its origins may be found in the BBC television serial filmed in 1968, also on the Worth Valley line. In February of that year, the director for the seven part serial, Julia Smith (subsequently the producer for 'EastEnders') was given a diesel railbus ride on the line and agreed that the location was eminently suitable. On Monday 25th March 1968, the complete BBC unit arrived and spent ten hectic days filming. Society members were kept equally busy setting up a fake signal near Oxenhope and sprucing up Oakworth station. This was shortly before the Railway was re-opened and Oakworth station required eight broken windows to be replaced, whilst gas lamps needed new mantles and lanterns. In addition, the station was painted and the fence repaired. Weeds adorned much of the area and these had to be cleared. Quite apart from all this, the three engines, Sir Berkeley, Joem, and No. 31 were prepared for three days of steam engine activity. On Sunday 12th May 1968, the first of the episodes was screened at 5.25pm. An excited crowd of Society members gathered around a television set in Haworth shed. This was, after all, the first real use of our Railway for a nationwide television programme and we were sure that the black and white film would provide a creditable record of our efforts. We all thought the programme quite splendid.

**Enter Mr Jeffries** - What we did not know was that watching the serial was Lionel Jeffries, the character actor of dozens of British feature films and the occasional big budget spectacular such as 'Chitty Chitty Bang Bang'. His daughter persuaded him to purchase the cinema screen rights and, because he was keen to make his directorial debut, Lionel Jeffries enthusiastically wrote the script and submitted it to Elstree Studios. As the British film industry lurched through another crisis, a new chief executive arrived at the studios in the form of Bryan Forbes, who had already worked with Lionel Jeffries. He like the script, rejected the idea of turning it into a musical, and allocated money for production as part of a ten film programme.

**Inspection and Approval** - Armed with studio approval, the new director obtained details of our Railway from the BBC and arranged to walk the line, together with producer Bob Lynn and your author. On a fine autumn day in 1969, the line was scrupulously examined and the principal locations were chosen. It was on this convivial occasion that Lionel Jeffries was persuaded to let Oakworth station retain its identity rather than use the name Meadow Vale, as in the BBC series. When the film was exhibited, this helped enormously in pinpointing the location, which in turn gave such a boost to our passenger figures. Subsequently, many more people made the journey to the Worth Valley to draw up plans for the filming. These included art director John Clarke and cameraman Arthur Ibbetson – the latter's credits included 'Where Eagles Dare' and 'Anne of a Thousand Days'. He had started his distinguished career as a clapper boy on David Lean's 1945 film 'Brief Encounter', centred, as readers may recall, on a railway station and, in fact, filmed at Carnforth. Sound was recorded by long standing railway enthusiast Peter Handford.

**Filming Commences** - Organisation for the feature film was more sophisticated than for the BBC production. Filming took longer, used more trains more frequently, and involved a much larger budget, though at £350,000 it was relatively economical by 1970 standards. When all the demands of the script had been defined, they were entered into a programme of filming called a 'crossplot'. This diagrammatic record commenced on Monday 6th April with filming of exteriors of a London villa, and concluded on Friday 12th June with interior shots in a railway tunnel. Listed for each day were the location, artists required, 'cabs, carriages, gigs & carts', trains, and the scene numbers to be filmed. In all, there were 15 studio days at Elstree and 39 location days, most of which were on the Worth Valley Railway, though Haworth village, the Parsonage and Wycoller hamlet were also used.

**The Trains** - Various types of train were discussed and three basic types evolved for different roles in the film.

ABOVE - The ex-GWR pannier tank No. L89 was to be the warm, friendly engine with the smart coaches painted in cream and dark maroon coupled to the wood-grained director's saloon in which the Old Gentleman rode so serenely - Photo: Robin Lush

ABOVE - The local train comprised a rather heterogeneous collection of four and six wheeled coaches and was hauled by Manchester Ship Canal locomotive No. 67 – Photo: Robin Lush

BELOW - The Barton Wright tender engine No. 957 was painted green and meant to be a rather fierce express engine, feared by all. So fierce in fact that its thunder and noise cause the landslide which is the centre-piece of the film, and it creates an opportunity for the children to save the following train from disaster – Photo: Robin Lush

Why the KWVR? – At the time, our Railway was the only preserved stretch of line which could provide such a wide range of rolling stock and working locomotives. All those chosen were of Victorian design and, whilst the express seemed a little on the slow side – indeed a mild joke was incorporated into the script to account for this – a branch line with a 25mph speed limit simply could not provide express train speeds. All the liveries used had their basis in contemporary illustrations and were adapted to the needs of the story. Liveries for coaches and locomotives were relatively straightforward. The major problem was getting the relevant trains marshalled each night, prior to filming the following day. If a train was filmed moving left to right at Oakworth station and was subsequently filmed at Haworth, the whole train had to be reversed, because the platform is on the other side of the line. This meant turning the engine at Shipley triangle and changing the coaches to match. Mercifully this was a rare occurrence, but British Rail provided facilities when needed with great efficiency. Whatever the situation, marshalling for the next day's filming rarely concluded before midnight and, if a big engine like the 'N2' was needed, lighting up commenced around 4am so as to be ready for an 8am start. The unit call was normally for 8.30am at the location and daily call sheets were issued detailing all the requirements from teaspoons to trains. When steam engines and trains were not required, but filming was taking place along the line, a diesel railbus took people and equipment to the spot. Alternatively this would be left to D226 plus a wagon and electrical generating equipment to power the arc lights invariably used, even though the weather throughout was superb.

ABOVE - The 'Scotch Express' comprising LNER 'N2' 0-6-2 No. 4744 and four bogie coaches whirls through Oakworth station – Photo: Brian Baker

A major location away from the stations was the landslide constructed on the bank in the cutting below Mytholmes tunnel. In the BBC version, a small tree was carried on the locomotive buffer beam to the bend near Oxenhope and supplemented with branches. The cinema version had something rather more spectacular. Three long steel channels were placed in the hillside with three short vertical tubes located in each. These were drawn up the hillside by cables and released to slide down as required. In the two outside tubes were placed small trees and, in the centre one, a rather special fibreglass tree made by the art department at Elstree. On the day of filming, when the centre tree reached its lowest point, the hinged base caused the trunk to fall over whilst, simultaneously, the 40 tons of Fuller's earth and gravel piled up behind sleepers at the bottom of the cutting were exploded, causing this mixture to slide across the track. It was all very expensive and, to this viewer, not particularly effective on the screen. Moreover, there was no opportunity for retakes once the charges were detonated. Perhaps a large tree across the track might have been more realistic and the money saved could have been spent on the canal sequence, where the three children rescue a baby from a burning barge. A location on the Leeds-Liverpool canal near the Fisherman's Inn at Wagon Lane, Bingley, was picked out but, sadly, abandoned because of lack of money.

The Film and its Makers – 'The Railway Children' was, even in 1970, a relatively rare phenomenon; a British financed production using United Kingdom locations which, together with vivacious performances from the leading players, Bernard Cribbins, Dinah Sheridan and William Mervyn and the three children, Jenny Agutter, Sally Thomsett and Gary Warren, created a warm hearted evocation of the more pleasant aspects of late Victorian England. It was the most successful of the ten films made during Bryan Forbes's reign at Elstree. Certainly, a competent directorial debut by Lionel Jeffries, it perhaps lacked the necessary emphasis on the trains which are, after all, the centre-piece of the film. This is not merely my prejudice. When compiling the film, editor Teddy Darvas had to arrange for a further day's filming to provide more engine shots for the averted crash sequence. More film was also needed of the 'Scotch Express' but alas by July the 'N2' had burst a boiler tube and was not available.

"The Green Dragon" near Haworth.                     photo: G. W. Morrison

**You can ride on the railway used by**

# "The Railway Children"

E.M.I.'s fine production of "The Railway Children" was filmed on the Worth Valley Railway which runs for five miles between Keighley in Yorkshire through Oakworth and Haworth (home of the Brontes) to Oxenhope.

You can see the engines and coaches actually used in the film and ride on the railway used by the children!

BELOW. Oakworth Station during filming—it is still kept as it was decorated for the film.

Released in December 1970, with a premier in London on 21st December and in Keighley soon after at the then Ritz cinema, where it played to packed houses, the film provided a real stimulus for our Railway. Nothing was left to chance and leaflets spelling out the location and services of the line where distributed wherever 'The Railway Children' played and Society members could gain access. Our Railway has been associated with this, by now, perennial cinema and television favourite ever since, and recently a touring stage play has been going the rounds, performed by the Birmingham Repertory Company and playing in the provinces to packed houses. Valuable publicity and input was made available by the Railway to this also. People still ask where the railway children lived (at Bent's Farm, Oxenhope), though they watched the trains near Oakworth by cinematic sleight of hand. Renewed interest in this admirable production will, once again, provide a stimulus to passengers and membership.

LEFT – KWVR publicity handout from 1970
Photo: KWVR Archives

# Edith Nesbit

'The Railway Children' author, Edith Nesbit, was born in 1858 at 38 Lower Kennington Lane in Kennington, London. The daughter of John Collis Nesbit, she was the youngest of five children and known to her family as 'Daisy'.

She spent her early years moving between France and England, unhappily attending a succession of boarding schools. In 1871 the family moved back to England and rented Halstead Hall in Kent where Edith and her brothers used to play near the railway line – a memory which was to inspire her future writing.

At the age of 21 and while seven months pregnant, Edith married bank clerk Hubert Bland. They shared a love of poetry and collaborated on many projects throughout a turbulent relationship where both partners openly conducted extra-marital affairs. Apart from her own two children, she brought up several that Bland fathered with his mistresses.

They were both socialists and involved in the Fabian Society from its inception - even naming one of their children Fabian after their joint interest. Nesbit befriended several of its members, including George Bernard Shaw (with whom she had an affair) and H.G. Wells. Adopting a nonconformist style, she cut her hair short, smoked heavily and wore less restrictive clothing than Victorian fashion dictated. Inspired by the Fabians' ideals, she wrote and lectured on socialism throughout the 1880s.

When Bland's business ventures failed, Nesbit became the main breadwinner and undertook other work to finance their growing household. She became a successful children's writer with novels including The Story of the Treasure-Seekers (1899), The Wouldbegoods (1901), Five Children and It (1902), The Phoenix and the Carpet (1904), The Railway Children (1906), and The Enchanted Castle (1907). Hubert Bland also collaborated with Nesbit on her writing, much of it being serialised in the 'London Weekly Dispatch' under the alias 'Fabian Bland'.

After the death of Hubert Bland in 1914, Edith married ship's engineer Thomas Tucker. She continued to write children's books but years of heavy smoking took their toll and she succumbed to lung cancer in 1924 at the age of 65, having published a total of 44 novels.

'The Railway Children' is probably the best known of Nesbit's many children's stories and was originally serialised in 'The London Magazine' during 1905 and published in book form in 1906, since which it has never been out of print. The best known version of the story is undoubtedly Lionel Jeffries' 1970 film and it is of note that the original episodic nature of the story remains evident in the film.

The Edith Nesbit Society ('www.edithnesbit.co.uk') aims to celebrate the life and work of the author and her friends with talks, publications, and a regular newsletter. The Society was the inspiration of Nicholas Reed, who became its first Chairman and long thought a wider audience should be aware of Nesbit's great contribution to children's literature.

# The Railway Children at the BBC _____

BBC TV has broadcast four serialisations of 'The Railway Children'. In 1951 Dorothea Brooking produced an adaptation which went out on Tuesday evenings in 8 episodes of 30 minutes each. The live programmes were not recorded but their popularity led to a remake later that year as four 60 minute episodes using largely the same cast and a mix of new and original material.

In 1957 a completely new version was produced by Dorothea Brooking which remained faithful to the earlier adaptation but included more location filming and railway scenes shot around Baynards station in Surrey on the old Guildford to Horsham line. It was broadcast nationwide and gained the rare honour of featuring on the cover of Radio Times - Photo: BBC World

In 1968 a new seven part serialisation of the story was broadcast which featured a young Jenny Agutter in the role of Bobbie and railway scenes filmed on the K&WVR. Although the production now feels a little dated, it is certainly a charming and faithful interpretation of the story and is the only version of the series currently available on DVD.

ABOVE - A youthful Jenny Agutter is seen here clinging to the station clock with other members of the cast and crew. Below her is the series Director Julia Smith who went on to find fame as the co-creator and Producer of EastEnders - Photo: Ken Roberts

ABOVE - Oakworth was renamed 'Meadow Vale' for the BBC series - Photo: Yorkshire Post

BELOW - Jenny Agutter with Gillian Bailey and Neil McDermott - Photo: Hubert Foster

# The film cast

Producer: Robert Lynn   Director: Lionel Jeffries   Screenplay: Lionel Jeffries
Music: Johnny Douglas   Director of Photography: Arthur Ibbetson B.S.C.

Photo: Howard Malham

| | |
|---|---|
| Mother | Dinah Sheridan |
| Mr Perks | Bernard Cribbins |
| The Old Gentleman | William Mervyn |
| Father | Iain Cuthbertson |
| Bobbie | Jenny Agutter |
| Peter | Gary Warren |
| Phyliss | Sally Thomsett |
| Doctor | Peter Bromilow |
| Ruth | Ann Lancaster |
| Shabby Russian | Gordon Whiting |
| Aunt Emma | Beatrix Mackey |
| Mrs Perks | Deddie Davies |
| Bandmaster | David Lodge |
| Jim | Christopher Witty |
| Viney | Brenda Cowling |
| Cart Man | Paddy Ward |
| Photographer | Eric Chitty |
| Maid | Sally James |
| C.I.D. Man | Dominic Allen |

# "The pretty life at Edgecombe Villa" _____

Some of the opening scenes were shot at Elstree's Borehamwood studio, while others used an empty house in Hampstead which was dressed with period fittings under the expert eye of Art Director John Clark. Here we meet the Waterbury family, Ruth the Maid, Great Aunt Emma and Potts the dog. The children live a happy life until one fateful day when two grim-faced gentlemen call to see Father. To their great horror he is arrested and taken away and life becomes very different indeed. Mother subsequently tells the children that Father has been unexpectedly called away on business and arranges for the strict Aunt Emma to help out for a while before she goes abroad to work as a Governess. The days that follow are very strange, with Mother away for long periods. Then one day she returns with important news; they must be very brave and 'play at being poor for a while'. She has made arrangements for them to move to a 'darling little house' in the country. Old and picturesque, it stands next to a sleepy old railway line ........................

ABOVE: Playing trains' between takes at Edgecombe Villa - Photo: Canal + Image UK

ABOVE: It's not all hard work. Dinah Sheridan and the 'Children' relax outside Elstree's studios in Borehamwood – Photo: Canal + Image UK

# "To a darling little house in the country" _____

*Following Father's arrest, the family move to the country and live in a house near the railway called 'Three Chimneys'*

ABOVE – The family arrive at Oakworth station – Photo: Canal + Image UK

Having struggled off the train with their heavy bags, the family meet a rather stern man driving a horse and cart who shows them the way up to 'Three Chimneys'

Photo: Canal + Image UK

# "Send our love to Father"

The children often ran down from Three Chimneys to wave to the train, asking it to "send our love to Father". This was a little bit of filming magic as the two locations are about two miles apart. Three Chimneys is above Oxenhope station, while the fence where the children waved is near Mytholmes tunnel between Haworth and Oakworth – Both photos: Canal + Image UK

# "Right away, Mr. Mitchell" _____

*KWVR volunteer and former Society Chairman, GRAHAM MITCHELL, describes how he landed a speaking role in the film.*

Back in 1970, I was in my fifth year as a junior master at Dudley Grammar School and was commuting to the Railway a couple of times a month to work as a volunteer. I'd been a Working Member since 1968 and having just qualified as a guard, I was very keen to do every turn that was available to me. It was therefore fortunate that the May half term holidays coincided with a call for volunteers to help with some filming work on the railway. I was available for the whole week, so it was my great luck to be chosen for the part of Guard in the film. Almost all of the sequences involving the train departures and arrivals from Oakworth were being shot during that particular week and there I was; as a newly passed out guard I got the opportunity.

ABOVE – Guard Graham Mitchell awaits the 'Right Away' at Oakworth while talking to 'The Old Gentleman' William Mervyn – Photo: Canal + Image UK

For my efforts I was paid the princely sum of seven pounds and fifteen shillings - a tidy sum given that my monthly net wage at that time as a qualified graduate teacher was only sixty pounds a month. I don't know if I was paid extra because I had a small speaking part, I was just glad to get the money and said "Thank you very much."

The excellent script is worthy of note, though certainly anyone familiar with Nesbit's book will understand that it bears little relationship to the words actually spoken in our classic film. This may be due in part to the close working relationship between Lionel Jeffries and Bernard

Cribbins who had acted together in many classic Boulting Brothers comedy films and clearly trusted each other as fellow professionals. This was Lionel's first film as a director and I think he simply trusted Bernard to get on with it. Most of the wonderful lines we remember like, "I've never seen anything more like a buttercup 'cepting it were a buttercup", "What's that squirrel doin' ont' table", and "It's all uphill to Scotland" are, I believe, all pure Cribbins ad-libs. I certainly never saw anything remotely resembling a script, though presumably the main actors all had them. Consequently, when we got to the train departure sequence, I was asked what we would normally do to take the train out. I explained that it was the duty of the station foreman to give the tip and discussed with Bernard what he would say as Mr Perks. He therefore says "Right away Mr Mitchell" and the guard responds "Thank you Mr Perks". It was actually made up on the spur of the moment, as were many of Bernard's lines, but it worked perfectly and we did it correctly because I explained how it should be done on a railway and we stuck to it.

My grand flourish of the green flag came about because they said, "Be slightly larger than life". Now as a shy and retiring 27 year old who had yet to develop the exuberant personality of later years, this did not come easily so I simply put a little extra flourish into that particular take and it seemed to work. The director liked it and that scene was in the can.

LEFT – William Mervyn 'The Old Gentleman' relaxes in between takes - Photo: Robin Higgins

Over the years, many journalists have asked, "What was it like working with Jenny Agutter?" They of course forget that Jenny and the other young actors Sally Thomsett and Gary Warren were relatively unknown then. The real stars at the time were comedy actor Bernard Cribbins and the fabulous Dinah Sheridan who had enjoyed a huge success a few years previously in the film 'Genevieve'. I also enjoyed sharing my train with the wonderful William Mervyn as The Old Gentleman, who was already well known through the hugely popular TV programme 'All Gas and Gaiters'. Cameras and microphones are a common enough sight in the Worth Valley these days but forty years ago it was a huge novelty to have a big film unit here and to see those big name stars here in our little villages and on our railway. People turned up just to see them, watch them filming and get their autographs, and the children were not really the focus of very much attention.

Continuity can throw up all sorts of problems. On the Sunday evening following my week on the railway, I got a phone call from the Assistant Director saying "We must have you back on set tomorrow as we've got to re-shoot some of your scenes". Now film companies live on a different planet to the rest of us and seemed unconcerned that I had to be back teaching at 9am on the Monday morning. Not wishing to incur the wrath of my very traditional headmaster, I suggested that the Assistant Director should make the approach. I was duly telephoned by my Headmaster who said, "Ah Mitchell, I have been approached by a theatrical personage who has asked me to allow you to take time off to appear in some sort of film, I suppose you'd better go then." I nervously thanked him and summoned a taxi to Wolverhampton station where I caught a train to Manchester Piccadilly, to be met by a chauffeur driven car and conveyed back to my parent's home. I appeared on set on Monday and all the scenes were re-shot. Sadly these all ended up on the cutting room floor, but that's life in the world of films. Incidentally, my headmaster didn't actually speak to me for about a month after this incident.

Anyone who has been involved in filming work will know that it can involve an awful lot of sitting around doing very little for an awfully long time. I recall sitting in the Old Gentleman's Saloon with William Mervyn awaiting instructions from the production crew. After about three hours, William was getting restless and walked down the line to accost Lionel Jeffries. 'Look, do you actually want us or not this morning - 'cos if you don't want us I'm taking this bloody train and were going to have some lunch'. With permission duly granted, the entire train repaired to Haworth whereupon William Mervyn, still in costume, made a beeline for the Royal Oak. "A flagon of ale for my companions, landlord, if you please". The train crew of course did not enjoy his hospitality for they were very definitely on duty, but I do remember William Mervyn and his friends enjoying a very merry afternoon.

ABOVE - Left to right: Jenny Agutter, Sally Thomsett, William Mervyn, Gary Warren, Bob Phizackerley (Driver), Graham Mitchell (Guard), Paul Waite (Fireman) - Photo: Ian Walker

The film's impact should not be underestimated. It enlivened the whole valley, and staff at Keighley's Ritz cinema had to seek out their 'House Full' notices when it was premiered there. There was a fantastic joy in and love of this film. It was our film, made in our valley, with our people, and on our railway. An elderly gentleman in Oakworth once said to me, "You know what's so great about that there film? It's got no drugs, no drinking, no sex, no bad language and no folk running round wi' no clothes on." And he was right for it's really a moral tale of good triumphing over evil, and it shows how a film can be a great film without having 'sex, drugs and rock and roll'. The film critic, Barry Norman, rated it the greatest British children's film ever made, and that's a fantastic compliment and a great triumph for this valley and for the railway.

My involvement with the filming was largely concentrated into that one week and it was clearly difficult to imagine how it would look on screen because you are just doing a series of short unconnected sequences in what is perhaps a two hour film. You don't understand the bigger picture until you finally see it on the screen. At the time it was a jolly romp with wonderfully interesting and famous people which caused great excitement in the area. I don't think any of us could have dreamt how it would turn out or the huge success it would become.

The impact upon the railway over the past forty years has been tremendous. I can think of no other single happening on the railway which has had such a big and lasting impact as the making of that film. I don't think that there was ever a day during the thirty-odd years that I was a working member on this railway when somebody didn't come up to me and mention the film. Some people have commented that I'm always talking about the film; that is simply not true. I never raise the subject, it is always other people who bring it up. I recall one man came up to me on Haworth Station after I retired and said, "I know you, you're that chap who used to be Graham Mitchell and you were in that Railway Children film".

ABOVE – William Mervyn with KWVR volunteer driver Nick Hellewell at Oxenhope station while the pannier tank takes water – Photo: Ian Walker

What people forget is that over the last 40 years, most of my age group on the railway have actually been involved in literally scores of short film scenes, mainly for TV. I and others have also "trod the boards" in lots of school and local 'Am Dram' productions, and still turn out for the occasional choice cameo role. So the fact that the 1970 film role continues to dog me after forty years remains something of a mixed blessing; I think it's called 'type-casting' so 'Thank you, Mr. Perks'.

# "The trees are walking down the bank" _____

*Creating the famous landslide scene caused more than a few headaches, not least for the driver of the 'Green Dragon' locomotive which set it off - MIKE GOODALL*

ABOVE – Mr. Goodall takes 'The Green Dragon' past the landslide site on one of the many runpasts demanded by the film makers – Photo: Robin Lush

Monday 8th June 1970 was already sweltering when I arrived in Haworth yard at 6am to get the steam locomotive No. 957 'The Green Dragon' ready for the day's filming. We were doing the landslide scene – the bit where the train charges through a cutting which then falls down. The yard was deserted and the loco which was supposed to set off at 8am, was not even lit up. This came as no great surprise as despite their elaborate plans, or 'shooting schedules' as I believe they call them, the film people often seemed to ignore everything and apparently make it up as they went along. To be fair, with actors having other commitments, getting them all together must have been a task to try the patience of Job. Thus when I found 957 standing idle, I assumed that there might have been an overnight change of plan. On the other hand, last minute changes of plan lead to many late-night-cum-early-morning shunts and perhaps the rest of the crew had just 'crashed out' through sheer exhaustion. To be on the safe side, I lit a fire in No. 957 and proceeded to get it ready. For two hours I had the place to myself, then at last came a sign that there was alternative life in Haworth. A gentleman approached and enquired if the train would be ready at the landslide site by 8.30am. I had to admire his sense of humour, for the chances of No. 957 even being on the boil by that hour were extremely remote. Sadly he was not joking and he went off to wait expectantly, if pointlessly, for the train at Mytholmes.

Enter Railway Chairman and film company 'Technical Consultant' Bob Cryer. Could I take the camera crew down to the site with D226? Err, no I could not. We had a golden rule that steam locomotives must not be left unattended if they were lit up, and I was the only person around. Bob vanished in the direction of the sleeping car to find the rest of the crew who, as I expected, had been shunting into the early hours. With assistance now at hand, I ferried the camera crew to the tunnel mouth.

Returning to Haworth, it was obvious that No. 957 was reluctant to make steam. With D226 hooked on to the front, the idle beast was dragged up and down the loop and persuaded to join the party. At last we were all ready and, some two hours behind schedule, we arrived on location. Having taken part in other filming epics, I was not entirely surprised to learn that nobody had really missed us. Had I not had the presence of mind to equip myself with 'The Times' the following hour or so would have been extremely boring, the only activity being that of the fibreglass tree sliding ponderously up and down the side of the cutting to the great amusement of the many locals who had gathered to watch the proceedings.

ABOVE – The famous fibreglass tree is securely lashed in place awaiting its starring role as members of the film crew are ferried around on the diesel railbus – Photo: Brian Baker

Time passed slowly by - then action at last. A gentleman bearing a walkie-talkie climbed on board. Could we run up past the cameras? 'Certainly – how fast shall we go?' 'As fast as you can' he replied. Unfortunately with the best part of 100 tons in tow, No. 957 did not want to go at all, at least not up the hill, which seemed a pity because that was where the cameras were situated. After several futile attempts to go forwards, I decided to set off back into Oakworth station. Off the curve, we stood a better chance of getting to grips with the rails.

With the chance to take a bit of a run at it, No. 957 now charged round Mytholmes curve and shot through the tunnel at a steady 30mph in full gear and second valve. Once clear of the tunnel, I stopped its gallop only for the walkie-talkie to burst into life. Could we do it again? Certainly – and again and again.

Over the next hour we made several 'flat out' runs using a boiler-full of water on each occasion. By the time lunch was taken, the tank was nearly empty so I asked the gentleman with the walkie-talkie what we were going to do afterwards. If we were to continue with the action, I would take the opportunity to go for water. The ether crackled and after a few moments he confirmed that we had finished filming. The afternoon was to be taken up with sound effects well away from the tunnel.

ABOVE – Setting up the landslide at Mytholmes cutting – Photo: Brian Baker

Lunch was a pleasant and unhurried affair taken in the yard of Vale Mill at Oakworth. No. 957 simmered under the trees South of the level crossing as we awaited our marching orders. Eventually the walkie-talkie returned – could we run past the cameras again? 'Pardon, I thought we had done that lot'. 'Oh no', came the reply, 'We want some more footage'. My language at this point would have got the blue pencil in the 'Bargees Weekly Chronicle'. We did a run, and then another. After the second run they asked for a third, but backing down towards Oakworth station we thought "What about water?" The injectors answered the question. One coughed, spluttered and failed to restart, followed almost immediately by the other. Now with a heavy train, an empty tank, a half empty boiler, and the nearest water supply two steeply climbing miles away, one can do one of two things: ditch the train and run like hell to the water supply, or throw the fire out. We opted for the former course of action.

As we uncoupled the train in Oakworth station, the walkie-talkie man became very agitated. Could we not wait a few minutes whilst he found out what was happening? 'No, we could not', came the stern reply. We had run right out of minutes and what was happening was quite simple; we were going for water, with or without him. He got off and we departed. No. 957 fairly galloped towards Mytholmes where a number of people were disporting themselves around the tunnel mouth – that mobile tree again. A series of frantic crows on the whistle persuaded them to clear the track. Through the tunnel, past Haworth to the welcoming sight of Oxenhope and the water tank.

ABOVE – The children race to save the train from disaster – Photo: Robin Higgins

With the boiler now empty, the burning question was would No. 957's often troublesome lifting injectors start again? They had been on their best behaviour all day but a spell of idleness in the scorching heat of the afternoon was just the sort of thing to make them play silly so-and-sos. With the water descending full bore into the tank, I tried the right hand injector. No cough, no splutter – it sang away as if it had never been off. The left hand one followed suit.

With the boiler and tank filled, we set off back. As we approached Haworth, someone suggested a wash in the porter's room. After a day of heat and grime, this sounded like a good idea. Then someone else suggested an ice cream so we paused on the platform. Having removed the encrusted dirt, and with an ice lolly clutched firmly in my hand, I emerged from the porters room and bumped into irate Railway boss Brian Baker. The film company were paying us good money and here we were idling our time away when we should have been filming. Gesticulating fiercely with my ice lolly, I pointed out that if the so-and-so film company could not make their so-and-so minds up as to what they were doing from one side of the lunch break to the other, then hard so-and-so lines. What was more, if Lionel Jeffries had any complaints, I would be only too pleased to tell him so to his face. Brian departed, and so did I.

Passing Mytholmes, guess what they were playing with? Correct in one – the mobile tree was still sliding up and down the side of the cutting. We reached Oakworth station and you would have thought that we had never left the place. Train? What train? Who wants a train anyway? We spent a pleasant hour or three in the sunshine of a perfect June afternoon and then, with the imitation tree securely parked for the night, made our way back to Haworth yard.

ABOVE – The fibreglass tree is erected above the timber retaining wall – Photo: Robin Lush

ABOVE – 'The trees are walking down the bank' – Photo: Robin Lush

BELOW – Bobbie waves her Red Flannel Petticoat to stop the train from running into the landslide. The whole scene was filmed in reverse and if you watch the film closely you can actually see the smoke going back into the locomotive's chimney – Photo: Brian Baker

# "The hound in the red jersey" _____

*HOWARD MAIS recalls his role as an 'extra' in the paperchase scene. This article first appeared in 'Down Your Way' magazine and is reprinted here with their kind permission.*

In March 1970 the tedium of preparing for ordinary level examinations for the fifth form at Roundhay Grammar School in Leeds was lifted when our English Language teacher, John Shuttleworth, told us that extras were being sought for the forthcoming filming of 'The Railway Children' in and around Oakworth and that if anyone was interested they should let him know and attend a selection meeting after school. To this day I do not know why our school and form were chosen for this, but it did cause a certain amount of envy among friends.

Having keenly put my name forward I attended the meeting a couple of evenings later. The Director and Screenplay Writer, former comedy actor Lionel Jeffries, came to the school with one of his colleagues and we were told that they were looking to choose "Twenty lads of assorted shapes and sizes" to participate in the paper chase scenes.

ABOVE – The runners enter the tunnel – Photo: Canal + Image UK

Being 6 feet 6 inches tall I had no trouble in meeting the assorted shape and size criteria and so some weeks later myself and nineteen class mates found ourselves being picked up by coach from near the school in the early morning. We did not go straight to Oakworth but instead diverted to the Merrion Centre Hotel to pick up others who would be involved with the film. These people turned out mainly to be extras as well, but from within the acting profession. Of course the stars of the film were transported in chauffeur-driven cars and were not expected to share a coach with twenty schoolboys.

When we arrived at Oakworth our changing rooms turned out, most appropriately, to be the compartments of an unused railway carriage. We were all provided with a set of black or white knickerbockers and a multi-coloured rugby shirt and soon got ourselves changed and ready.

The experience was great fun and we spent, if I recall correctly, three full days in Oakworth over a couple of weeks. The weather on all the days we were there was fine and sunny and I presume that those days had been chosen on the basis of reliable weather forecasting. Much of our time, though, was spent watching other scenes being filmed, including the famous avalanche scene, rather than being filmed ourselves.

ABOVE – The frightened children try to rescue the injured runner – Photo: Canal + Image UK

Our main piece of action was when the paper chase went through a tunnel. One of the smaller lads among us, Ozzie, was chosen to be the hare and as he had a line to say in the film he was paid twice as much as the rest of us. Very soon we were filming the scene in which Ozzie spoke his line of "Let me pass please" to the Railway Children before he entered the tunnel. The rest of us watched a number of takes before it was our turn to be filmed running down the railway banking past the Railway Children and disappearing into the tunnel. Again there were a number of takes and none of us really knew what was making one take acceptable and others not. We were then able to watch the filming of the actor who was running well behind the rest of us entering the tunnel. In the story he fell and broke his leg in the tunnel only to be saved by the Railway Children before a train could arrive and run him over.

We didn't have to run through the tunnel but our next scene involved queuing up to run out of it and up the steep banking. Again there were a number of takes and for the last one we were asked to collapse with exhaustion when part way up the banking. We all then displayed what we naively believed to be our superb acting talents by falling on the banking, usually as if shot by an unseen sniper. With the benefit of hindsight it was realised that this had been purely for the amusement of the film crew who probably never even set the cameras rolling. There were certainly no dying paper chasers to be seen when the film eventually came out.

We then had to do some long distance running shots through the village and across the countryside, crossing fields and leaping over dry stone walls. One of our classmates, Ox, didn't leap high enough and partly demolished one of the walls to great amusement but this comedy moment did not make the final cut.

LEFT – With the train due at any time, runner Jim lies trapped inside the tunnel with a broken leg

Photo: Canal + Image UK

The last thing I recall us doing was some sound recording. We were assembled on the platform of Oakworth station and asked to run on the spot. We were told that when we were pointed to we should say something that we might spontaneously have said whilst running in a real paper chase. However the kind of things we were prone to say as 1970s schoolboys were not always representative of what Edwardian schoolboys might have said in the same circumstances. Nevertheless some of the more acceptable comments can be heard during the tunnel scenes.

Nineteen of us were paid £5 per day for our efforts whilst Ozzie received £10 per day. This was good and very welcome money for schoolboys in 1970. We were also fed for free from the mobile catering units. However to this day I do regret not having done a deal for royalties in the light of how often the film is screened, especially as that proved to be the beginning and end of my acting career.

When the film was released we all went to the cinema on the opening night to see it. To say we had spent three days on set it was surprising how short the scenes we appeared in turned out to be. We were on screen for a total of about fifty seconds out of the film's running time of approximately one and three quarter hours. As a consequence I do not think that every one of the twenty of us actually appeared on screen. I was pleased to see that I did but these days very few people can recognise me unless I point myself out, such have been the ravages of time on my physique and appearance.

# "Excellent Hastwell"

Most people probably didn't even notice him as the Butler in the Old Gentleman's Saloon but Ken Hastwell, a retired former cinema projectionist, has an impressive list of acting roles on his CV. Apart from his brief appearance in 'The Railway Children' Ken has appeared as an extra in Coronation Street, Heartbeat, Only Fools and Horses, Emmerdale Farm, Open All Hours, Ripping Yarns, Sherlock Holmes, The Flaxton Boys, Taggart and Yanks. He even appeared in Last of the Summer Wine as Compo's stunt double.

Now aged 83 and living in Leeds, Ken has fond memories of working on 'The Railway Children'. "I spent five weeks at the Railway playing a waiter who served some wine to William Mervyn. It took a while to get used to the movement of the train while pouring the wine but it was a most enjoyable time" – Photo: Ken Hastwell

ABOVE – Butler Ken Hastwell waits inside the saloon as the school boy runner Jim returns home having recovered from his injuries – Photo: Canal + Image UK

# The Old Gentleman's Saloon _____

*The 'Old Gentleman's Saloon' from 'The Railway Children' has a history of railway use stretching back nearly 140 years, as owner CHRIS LAWSON recalls.*

ABOVE – The saloon basks in the sun at Oxenhope station – Photo: Chris Lawson

It was originally built in 1871 as a 4 wheeled smoking saloon for the Stockton and Darlington Railway (S&DR). Three years previously, Parliament had passed legislation requiring the railways to provide separate smoking accommodation for their passengers. In response, the S&DR ordered the construction of two smoking saloons at Darlington, of which this was one, for use on their long distance routes, mainly over Stainmore to Tebay and Penrith. Although taken over by the North Eastern Railway (NER) in 1863, the S&DR operated as a separate entity until 1876, when all rolling stock was incorporated into the NER. At this time the Saloon became No 1661 under the NER numbering system.

It continued in use as a smoking saloon until the early 1880s, when it was put on to a 6 wheeled frame and converted to become the Inspection Saloon for the Locomotive Superintendent of the NER. It was based at Gateshead Locomotive Works and paired with locomotive No 66 'Aerolite'. As such it was used by the Locomotive Superintendent as his private train to carry out inspections of the premises – locomotive works, engine sheds, carriage and wagon works – and staff for whom he was responsible across the NER area. The precise date of its conversion is not clear, but it is likely to have been used by Edward Fletcher and Archibald McDonnell and certainly by the Worsdell brothers, TW and then Wilson.

1900 saw its use on a Royal Train from York to Newcastle, conveying the then Prince (later Edward VII) and Princess of Wales for the laying of the foundation stone of what is now the Royal Victoria Infirmary.

By 1904, Wilson Worsdell had decided that the Locomotive Superintendent should in future be known as the Chief Mechanical Engineer (CME) and that his Inspection Saloon should be upgraded. It was therefore lengthened and placed on a bogie frame, providing a saloon seating 15 with armchairs and a meeting table, a toilet, guard/stewards compartment with wine rack and cool box, and a kitchen with crockery and cutlery cupboards – a self contained office on wheels. This internal layout is retained in the Saloon to the present day.

On Worsdell's retirement in 1910, the Saloon was moved to Darlington North Road, along with 'Aerolite' and the NER Dynamometer Car, and was re-allocated to the Assistant CME, A.C. Stamer. He continued to use it, through the Grouping and the formation of the London and North Eastern Railway (LNER) in 1923 when it was renumbered 21661, until his retirement at the end of 1933. At that time, 'Aerolite' was withdrawn for preservation and can now be seen at the National Railway Museum in York, and the Saloon was moved to York Carriage Works where, in 1934, it was converted to its present external condition with large picture windows.

ABOVE – Awaiting passengers for the Cream Tea Specials - Photo: Chris Lawson

Subsequently it was first used by Edward Thompson and then by Arthur Peppercorn as their Inspection Saloon while they were based at Darlington, before being moved to York on the nationalisation of the railways at the beginning of 1948. Here it became the Inspection Saloon for the Chief Regional Officer of the new North Eastern Region of British Railways (BR) and was renumbered E902179E. It was finally transferred to the Signal and Telecommunications (S&T) Department at York in the early 1950s, where it was used by the S&T Engineer, Arthur Wigram, for his inspections of signalling schemes across the Region.

By March 1969, the Saloon was deemed surplus to requirements and was purchased privately by the late John Dawson in March 1969 from BR for £500. It was moved to the preserved and newly reopened Keighley and Worth Valley Railway (KWVR) in West Yorkshire in May and, in 1970, became the 'Old Gentleman's Saloon' in 'The Railway Children' film, in which William Mervyn played the 'Old Gentleman'.

Normally based on the KWVR, as an ex-S&DR vehicle it was exhibited at the Stockton and Darlington Railway 150 Anniversary celebrations at Shildon in August 1975. For this it was put through Doncaster BR Engineering Works where it was restored to the varnished teak livery in which it can be seen today. From May to October 1977 the Saloon was on hire to the Derwent Valley Light Railway at York for the operation of a steam hauled passenger service on this otherwise freight only line. The Saloon has also been on display at the National Railway Museum in York on three separate occasions, and in 1991 visited the North Yorkshire Moors Railway as part of the celebrations of the 25th Anniversary of the North Eastern Locomotive Preservation Group.

Now owned privately by Chris Lawson, it is normally kept in the Carriage Shed at Oxenhope, but it does see use on filming assignments, special trains (including a visit to the Railway by the Duke of Kent in 2008), and on Vintage Train weekends during the summer when cream teas are served on board to passengers who have booked for a round trip on the line. In 2010 the Saloon is planned to play a major role in the celebrations, both on the KWVR and elsewhere, to mark the 40th Anniversary of the making of 'The Railway Children' film.

ABOVE – The saloon passes the film crew near Mytholmes tunnel – Photo: Bill Black

# The brass band

In the words of the much missed Eric Morecambe, "All the right notes, but not necessarily in the right order".

Members of the Haworth Brass Band put in a memorable performance during the presentation scene at Oakworth while under the baton of their increasingly frustrated bandmaster, played by the actor David Lodge.

Photo: Haworth Band

Haworth Brass Band continues to flourish and when additional scenes were required for the newly remastered DVD version of the film, we were delighted to welcome back some of the band members who took part in the 1970 filming – Photo: Jim Shipley

# "Daddy, my Daddy"

*Now that forty years have passed since Jenny Agutter uttered those immortal words, perhaps it is time to lift the lid off the real events of 1970 – MIKE GOODALL reveals all.*

The final scheduled day's shooting was for the 'Daddy, My Daddy' scene where father returned home from prison – and it was a complete farce. Mind you, after five weeks of swapping and changing, it was perhaps inevitable that the film crew would end up with the wrong train.

ABOVE – The memorable reunion scene at Oakworth station - Photo: Canal + Image UK

The film trains consisted of 'The Green Dragon', the 'Scotch Flyer', the 'Old Gentleman's Train' and the local train which apparently came from Wakefield. The latter consisted of Manchester Ship Canal 0-6-0T No. 67 and a selection of four or six wheeled coaches and had been specially provided with a continuous pipe beneath the footboards from which copious amounts of steam could blow across the platform. When Daddy returned from his unfortunate encounter with the prison service, the idea was that he should emerge from the midst of this steam into the arms of his unbelieving elder daughter. Unfortunately they asked for - and got - the Old Gentleman's Train. Not only was there no leaky pipe from which steam could issue profusely, but the Old Gentleman's engine, Pannier L89, did not even have steam heating equipment.

When the mistake was discovered, several things happened almost simultaneously. One group of people, no doubt with an eye on their future employment in the film industry, descended on the unfortunate Lionel Jeffries to let him know it wasn't their fault. Others, a little less sanguine, aired their superior knowledge by informing all and sundry that they knew it was the wrong train all along.

A special effects man attempted to salvage the day by sticking a long rubber hose on one of L89's injector overflow pipes and laying it under the train. Steam did blow out over the platform until the injector overheated and burst a joint. Steam then blew all over L89. A random selection of expletives persuaded the man that his suggestion to repeat the experiment with the remaining injector did not meet with the approval of the train crew.

Left – Mike Goodall's charge, pannier tank L89, which got the film crews all steamed up during filming at Oakworth

Photo: Robin Higgins

Considering that he was the Director, Lionel Jeffries appeared to take the whole thing most calmly. He had contingency funds for 'hidden extras' so could we come back the following day with the correct train? The following day we turned up at Oakworth with the correct train plus L89. Two engines with only one crew; highly irregular, so could we have double pay? I regret to say we are still waiting for this. With L89 dumped in the back siding, we did the emotional arrival, complete with steam clouds. The train was then swapped for L89. During the previous day's debacle, Lionel had thought up an extra shot to heighten the drama of the landslide scene. Fasten a camera to the leading steps and let it run as the engine bore down on the petticoat-waving children. With the wheel revolving ponderously in front of the lens, we trundled off towards Damems for this last shot.

Additional footage was taken through the cab window and then I was back to Oakworth. Lionel Jeffries made a little speech thanking everybody and told them to 'break the set', by which we assumed that the whole affair was over. The film people started to load their equipment while we whilst we hooked up No. 67 and its train. The excitement over, we made our leisurely way back to Oxenhope to dump the train and water the engines. When we eventually arrived back in Haworth yard, we were accosted by some none-too-pleased individuals with a large pantechnicon. It was the costume department. For some obscure reason we had been fitted into some period garments and now they wanted them back. With the rest of the film crew half way to London by now, they were still stuck in the back of beyond awaiting the return of a train crew who could see no reason to rush and who, if the truth were known, had completely forgotten that they were wearing somebody else's trousers.

With their departure, Sleepy Hollow returned to normal. True, a camera crew did come back for some additional train shots, but that, as far as we were concerned, was the end of 'The Railway Children'. Or so we thought ...................

# "Conversationalising with the junior public" _

*KWVR volunteer DAVID PEARSON recalls his days as a short-trousered school boy and how he played a part in the famous 'Daddy, My Daddy' reunion scene.*

I was 15 when 'The Railway Children' was filmed and recall it very well indeed. I was still at school (St. Bede's in Bradford) and ached every day to get to the Railway so that I could see what was going on. It must have been filmed some time round the holidays (Easter I think) as I know that I spent a lot of full days at Oakworth and did all sorts of odd jobs around the place. One thing which sticks clearly in my memory is Lionel Jeffries calling out numbers when the train stopped with Mother arriving from Wakefield. Each number was a passenger in one of the Metropolitan Coaches and they popped out according to the numbers; it looks a bit false on the finished film and staged, and that's why.

ABOVE - Another shot is lined up at Oakworth station - Photo: Brian Baker

The landslide was fun. It had to be cleared up for the following weekend's services and could only be done once; it was a bit like watching 'The Bridge on the River Kwai', but it worked. We had the fake tree for years afterwards in Oakworth Yard and you can still see the place where the wall above Norman Feather's coal pile was demolished and rebuilt to allow Peter to come and steal the coal to keep Mother warm.

There was quite a lot of movement between Keighley and Shipley to turn locomotives on the triangle. It was very easy to arrange in those days. 957 was sent there a couple of times and somewhere I have some photographs of her standing in platform 3, in full GN & SR livery after having been returned by BR from such a trip. I never thought how much she would thirty years later, dominate my life.

On one very memorable occasion, we were hanging around Oakworth and William Mervyn (right) became bored. He shouted to Lionel Jeffries (below) something like "Do you need this bloody train Lionel?" to which he received a negative reply. I can recall the confidence and incredulity that I experienced as the incomparable Mervyn (he was already a hero to me from his role as the Bishop in 'All Gas and Gaiters') ordered the pannier tank and Old Gentleman's saloon full of us 'helpers' to Haworth where we decamped to the Royal Oak, Bill Mervyn in costume rapping on the bar and ordering "Two gallons for my Railway friends, landlord if you please". It's a daft tale I know, but one which made a most profound impression upon a very impressionable youth.

I suppose one of the daftest things I ever did was to find a script for the film, full of actor's annotations which had been thrown away in a bin in Haworth Yard, look at it and throw it away in turn; it would probably have been worth a bob or two now. It came from a row of coaches in the Yard (there was no New Shed there then) which were used as a wardrobe and dressing rooms for the extras.

The Hares and Hounds were posh kids from Roundhay Grammar School, which was a sequence I recall took a few days to film. For a time it looked as if the film crew would round up any handy adolescents from the valley to fill the extras' parts, but our hopes were dashed.

In the event, I did get a role. If you look at the very end of the film, as Father arrives and steam clears, you can see me closing the level crossing gates. Phil Slack, the then Oakworth Stationmaster ought to have done it, but he was away for some reason so I got my first ever paid job and the only cash that to this day, I have ever had as a result of my involvement in the Railway. A fiver was a fortune in those days and I recall I bought a book with it.

The scenes of the train heading towards the landslide were done much later, when the weather was very hot and it was our school summer holiday. Some might find it difficult to believe, but I cleaned the pannier tank on those days and got the odd footplate ride as a result. It was my first since BR days, when I had a run on an Ivatt tank on the Push & Pull service, so it really meant a lot to me.

It's all a lifetime away now but perhaps one day we will be able to do something like it all over again. One thing's for sure, I'll certainly never forget it all.

Photos: Robin Lush

# Costume and make up _____

*The film company set up a site office and costume department in some railway carriages in Haworth Yard. Long standing KWVR volunteer KEN ROBERTS was there and recalls many incidents which took place in 'his' carriages*

I had a few days off in May 1970 during the filming of 'The Railway Children', and upon entering Haworth Yard I noticed several coaches being set down into the old No. 4 road. I later learnt that they were to become the on-site headquarters of the film company. From memory, among the coaches were the Chatham brake, Pullmans 84 and 'Zena', the latter now forming part of the Orient Express rake. A day or so later I noticed that the local Electric Board had fixed up heating and lighting in all these coaches. That same evening, a few of us had a sneaky look inside them ..... wow. Edwardian clothes were hanging up from racks and spread all over the place. A couple of lads put on strange headgear such as bobbies helmets, pith helmets and pill box hats. A security firm called Wideawake was apparently employed to keep guard of things but was clearly not wide awake when the aforementioned capers took place. Wideawake's alsation dog had a sort of silent bark and could hardly walk – Photo: Brian Baker

The following day we again ventured into the coaches to find more interesting things. Inside the Chatham was a lady operating a huge washing machine. She told us that she went out East to do any washing during 'Lawrence of Arabia'. "By gum" said one of the lads, "I'll bet that machine got bunged up with sand". The lady did not think the remark was funny and said "Don't think I'm going to wash your lot's dirty overalls".

Going into the Pullmans and ploughing through Edwardian frocks and other frilly things, tail coats etc, we went into 'Zena' which, being a first class Pullman, had private cubicles at each end of the car. One was for Dinah Sheridan and the other was for Bernard Cribbins. In the centre of this car was a large board on which were written the names of the cast, the Producer and Director, and the Technical Director the late Bob Cryer. Now Bob was a movie buff and so got his name, at last, on the screen.

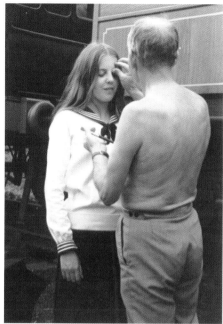

LEFT – Dinah Sheridan's costume receives attention in the elegant surroundings of the first class Pullman Car 'Zena' – Photo: Canal + Image UK

RIGHT – Sally Thomsett (Phyliss) receives attention from the Make-up Department in Haworth Yard – Photo: Robin Higgins

Some members of the Railway were asked to do fire-watching duties for a wage of £4 per person per night. That was good money in those days but the Railway's Council had decided that any member doing this work should hand back all, or at least 50%, of those earnings. £4 was also the amount paid to the lads from a school in Leeds for their part in the paper chase scene. On giving the lads the money, the School Master remarked, "That is the easiest money you will ever earn in your lives".

Down at Oakworth, one of the coach's droplight straps broke. Asking one of the film staff where I might get some strong thread, I was directed towards the Wardrobe Department. "See those fancy boys over there ….. that is the wardrobe department".

There was a short break in filming over the Whit weekend and the weather was nice and warm. One scene at Oakworth demanded a wet platform so out came the local fire brigade to provide torrential rain on demand. Chatting to Jenny Agutter at Oakworth, I asked if she had gone South with the rest of the crowd over Whit. I thought I heard her say "No, I have been to see my parents in St Helens". Methinks this lass is no snob.

To many of the onlookers, the star of the whole event was the film's Director Lionel Jeffries. Already well known as an actor, 'The Railway Children' was his first stint as Director. He usually arrived on the set at about 7am with a very big red scarf around him and an after-shave with an aroma not unlike The Famous Grouse or Arthur Bell – a splendid chap.

# Railway Children trivia _____

Sally Thomsett (left) was twenty when she played the part of twelve year old 'Phyliss'. She is actually two years older than Jenny Agutter, who played her older sister 'Bobbie' in the film.

'Roberta' is named after Berta Ruck, a close friend of E. Nesbit.

Sally Thomsett and Bernard Cribbins were both nominated for BAFTA awards for their performances in the film.

The film's music was written by Johnny Douglas. The theme song 'More than ever now' was even a top 100 hit for Al Martino.

The character of 'The Photographer' was played by Erik Chitty, who became famous as an elderly teacher in the popular TV comedy series 'Please Sir'.

The character of 'Mrs Perks' was played by Deddie Davies, who found fame with the superannuated pop group 'The Zimmers'. Their cover version of The Who's 'My Generation' successfully highlighted the plight of the elderly and made the charts in May 2007.

Jenny Agutter (right) and Christopher Witty played 'Bobbie' and 'Jim' in both the 1968 TV and 1970 film versions

In 2005, a stage musical version of the story was presented at Sevenoaks Playhouse in Kent, with a cast including Paul Henry (Benny from 'Crossroads') as Mr. Perks

Hundreds of built up wooden covers were created to hide the modern concrete sleepers in some of the close-up shots.

'The Between Maid' was played by a young actress called Sally James, who later found fame on the Saturday children's TV show TISWAS, which also starred Chris Tarrant. She now runs a successful children's clothing company in Cobham.

The Waterbury family's dog 'Potts' was called actually 'James' in Edith Nesbit's book.

'Peter' was played by Gary Warren (left), who also appeared in 'Z Cars' and 'Catweazle'. Now retired from acting, he lives and works in Canada.

Oakworth station had just been repainted, but the film company decided to apply a 'weathering' coat to make it look dull.

Photos: KWVR archives (centre), Robin Higgins (top & bottom)

# "Most extraordinary indeed"

*KWVR steam driver, NICK HELLEWELL, recalls his starring role with the Old Gentleman's Train, and how Lionel Jeffries' handkerchief saved the day.*

One of those perfect early summer mornings in 1970 found us chuffing gently up towards Oxenhope, with the 'put-put' of the vacuum pump on the pannier tank prompting my driver, Bob Phizackerley, to remark that we might have been anywhere on the Western Region of British Railways with a branch train to somewhere rural.

Our duty was to do whatever director Lionel Jeffries (pictured left) asked of us with this, the Old Gentleman's Train. Our pannier tank No. L89 of 1929 vintage, would have to come bursting out of Mytholmes tunnel an endless number of times with her train before the day was over. We had a man with a walkie-talkie on the footplate to give instructions like, "Stop", "Go", "Faster", "Slower", and also "Can you make it stay quiet now?" This latter request coming only minutes after him telling us, "We shall need a high speed run with plenty of noise and steam as soon as you can, driver".

We devoted a whole morning to this activity, watching the three children wave at us from the lineside fence. We also had to keep an eye on a man who ran along the line with a flag held aloft, allegedly at a similar speed to our own. We were fortunate in that the Old Gentleman (alias the late William Mervyn), sitting in the rear saloon carriage, seemed to have a thirst that coincided with our pannier - so with an influential word to Mr Jeffries, we were released to Oxenhope where water was taken. There then followed a rapid descent to Haworth where everyone (except me) followed the Old Gentleman's invitation to the Royal Oak. I loyally stuck to my post lest the pannier tank should have any silly ideas of her own. We shortly backed down to Mytholmes where, in true film company fashion, a feast had been laid out on tables above the tunnel.

The afternoon continued much as the morning, but here lies my ultimate claim to fame. When the time came to shoot the final run-past where all and sundry wave at the children to indicate their pleasure at the release of their father from prison, my handkerchief, after many hours on the footplate, proved to be inadequately white for waving. Lionel Jeffries loaned me his and that part of the film was in the can. – Photo: KWVR

# Lights, Camera, Action _____

*Hollywood comes to Haworth? – It certainly seemed that way during the glorious summer months of 1970 when the Railway was turned into a huge film set and Railway volunteers worked alongside the technicians and actors to bring Edith Nesbit's famous story to the silver screen*

ABOVE – Peter Bromilow (Doctor Forrest), Gary Warren (Peter), and Sally Thomsett (Phyliss) get lined up for another shot at Oakworth station – Photo: Peter Eastham

ABOVE – The fence at the south end of Mytholmes tunnel is where the children waved to the Old Gentleman on the train - Photo: Robin Lush

BELOW – The children at play between shots at Oakworth station – Photo: N.R. Knight

ABOVE: The children are presented with watches at Oakworth station following their brave actions in saving the train from disaster – Photo: Robin Lush

BELOW – Director Lionel Jeffries and crew on Oakworth platform – Photo: Robin Higgins

ABOVE: The film crew fix electrical cables between the coaches - Photo: Martin Welch

BELOW: Bob Cryer and Guy Henderson (right) look on as equipment is unloaded from a wagon hauled by the diesel railcar - Photo: Martin Welch

ABOVE – The pannier tank No. L89 is decorated for the final scenes – Photo: Martin Welch

BELOW – The crew and cast relax between takes. The Director and all of the major actors had their own personalised chair – Photo: Robin Higgins

# Lionel Jeffries

As this book was being prepared, we received the sad news that Lionel Jeffries had passed away on 19th February 2010 following a long illness. He was 83. He will be fondly remembered for his work on 'The Railway Children', but his career also included TV and stage work plus appearances in over 100 films, including Chitty Chitty Bang Bang, Two Way Stretch, The Wrong Arm of the Law, The Colditz Story, Doctor at Large, and Blue Murder at St Trinians,

ABOVE – Lionel Jeffries with Musical Director Johnny Douglas - Photo: Canal + Image UK

BELOW – Lionel and team while filming on Haworth Main Street - Photo: Canal + Image UK

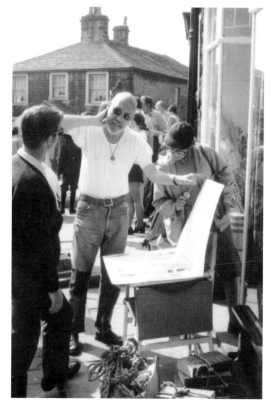

Chairman of the Keighley and Worth Valley Railway Preservation Society, Paul Brown, paid tribute to him, saying, "There have been many richly deserved tributes to Lionel Jeffries from the world of stage and screen, but volunteers on the K&WVR will always remember that it was his work with our Railway forty years ago that made our success possible. It made people realise that we were not just a group of eccentric amateurs doomed to inevitable failure, but that we had shown, at a time when local railways were being closed everywhere, that communities could take them over and run them successfully".

Paul added: "We will be celebrating the film's 40th anniversary during 2010 and will be taking time to remember Lionel Jeffries and all that he, along with a superb cast and crew, did for the future of this Railway. Thanks to him, people from all over the world still come to ride on our trains and visit Oakworth station. The world has lost a great actor and director, a true character, and a very fine gentleman"

ABOVE – Young actress Jenny Agutter gazes admiringly at Dinah Sheridan during preparation for filming of 'The End' scene at Ebor Lane near Haworth - Photo: Canal + Image UK

# "Perks must be about it"  _____

*Bernard Cribbins and his character of Mr Perks are now forever linked with Oakworth, as former Station Master JIM SHIPLEY recalls.*

Bernard Cribbins was already a well known and respected comedy actor when he played the part of Perks the Porter in 'The Railway Children'. He had appeared in several classic Boulting Brothers comedies and done everything from fighting Daleks with Dr Who to appearing in Coronation Street. He was even the voice of 'Tufty' in the 1960s road safety films and 'Buzby' in the Post Office Telephones adverts.

ABOVE – A proud Mr. Albert Perks with wife Nell and family – Photo: Canal + Image UK

In 'The Railway Children', his character of Mr. Perks was a proud and stubborn Yorkshireman who would not stand for any of that "charity nonsense" despite having a wife and family to support on his meagre pay from the Railway. He took great pride in his job and happily befriended the 'upper class' Waterbury family who had fallen on hard times. He helped sort out their problems and forgave occasional misdemeanours such as stealing coal from the station to keep mother warm. He offered presents of 'Sweet Briar' to the children's ill Mother and even had a small gift for Roberta's birthday. It was his well meaning gift of newspapers and magazines that led Roberta to realise the true extent of her father's plight. Perks was always there to offer friendly advice and act as a go-between in their adventures.

Forty years on, passengers still come to Oakworth station in search of Mr Perks and to watch today's staff operate the level crossing, pull the signals, and shout "Oakworth, Oakworth" in true 'Perks' fashion as the train pulls into the platform. They are never disappointed.

# "The End"

ABOVE - The famous scene at the end of the film where the cast wave to the camera was filmed at Ebor Lane Bridge near Haworth station - Photo: Canal + Image UK

BELOW - Once the official shots were finished, some local children decided to get in on the act, no doubt hoping to be spotted by a passing talent scout – Photo: KWVR